INTRODUCTION

Debt is so common in America that most people don't question it. It's woven into our homes, our cars, our education, and our everyday decisions. The system teaches us to borrow early, borrow often, and spend a lifetime paying for it. What most never see is how this cycle quietly controls their time, their energy, and their future.

The Power of No Debt is about breaking that control.

This book gives you the mindset and the mechanics to step out of the debt trap and into ownership. You'll learn the real difference between money and currency, how inflation steals your purchasing power, and why debt has become the modern form of financial slavery. More importantly, you'll learn how to build a life where your income works for you, not against you.

Freedom from debt isn't about perfection. It's about intention. It's the shift that turns pressure into peace, chaos into clarity, and survival into strategy. When you owe nothing, your decisions become stronger, your options expand, and your confidence rises.

This journey starts with awareness, grows with discipline, and ends with independence.

When you reclaim your financial power, you reclaim your life.

THE POWER OF NO DEBT

THE POWER OF NO DEBT

GARY HAYWOOD

GH
WOOD
LLC

Currency

vs

Money

Understanding the Difference

This knowledge separates those who live with control from those controlled by the system. In today's economy, where every decision carries a price, clarity about how value truly moves is essential.

Money represents value itself.

For anything to be considered *money*, it must serve three purposes:

Medium of Exchange
Store of Value
Unit of Account

...for you laymen,
Intrinsic Value

Currency (legal tender)

By contrast, **is the physical or digital form that represents money**, such as the US Dollar. It is currency not money itself.

Currency is **fiat**, meaning it holds value only because the US government deems it so.

A US dollar bill of *any* denomination has no intrinsic value, it is simply ink and paper.

This distinction is not well known or alluded to. When you understand the difference, you begin to recognize how the system operates, and how easily value can be manipulated.

Currency loses purchasing power through inflation; the more that's printed, the less each dollar buys. True money retains value only.

Purchasing Power

refers to the *value of* currency, money, anything used for barter or trade.

Money measures the real worth of currency, or how much you can actually buy with it.

It's a key concept in economics, finance, and monetary policy, because it links prices, income, and inflation.

For **Consumers:** Determines real living standards.
For **Businesses:** Supply/Demand cost structures.

For The Federal Reserve: The ULTIMATE power and control dynamic.

Debt, when viewed honestly, is not just a financial transaction it's a transfer of power.

You *borrow*; you *repay*. In reality, debt often binds one person's future to another's profit.

Debt is a modern form of **SLAVERY,** dressed in the language of opportunity.

The system profits not from your success, but from your ongoing obligation.

Must work to pay bill's

Breaking free from that cycle begins with awareness.

When you control debt instead of serving it, you reclaim your time, your energy, and your autonomy.

Because when you owe nothing, you cannot be controlled. Owe nothing. Own everything.

That is the discipline of independence, built through planning, purpose, and ownership.

The Debt-Free Mindset

A debt-free life is not merely a financial goal it is a state of clarity and strength. It's waking up without the weight of obligation and knowing your income belongs to you.

Freedom from debt doesn't mean you stop working... it means your work finally starts working *for you.*

When debt disappears, power becomes available as if a veil has been lifted. Your vision clears and financial decisions become intentional and not reactive. Peace replaces pressure while flexibility replaces fear.

Subtraction no longer, instead, addition and eventually multiplication of your income.

This lifestyle is not about having everything; it's about owning what you have and owing nothing to anyone. It is a mindset, a discipline, and a declaration of self-ownership.

EPILOGUE

Closing this chapter isn't an ending, it's a hand-off. Every step you've taken through these pages connects directly to the larger movement. The principles you've explored here don't live alone. They're part of a bigger ecosystem designed to sharpen your thinking, strengthen your discipline, and push you toward a debt-free, self-directed life.

Self EMS: Implementing Perpetual Success laid the foundation, mindset, energy, and consistency. That book was your ignition switch, the spark that taught you how to build momentum from the inside out.

The Haywood Saga (a memoir') pulled back the curtain and revealed the real journey behind the message, the setbacks, the transformation, the faith, and the brick-by-brick climb. It showed that the path to freedom isn't theory. It's lived experience.

Mastering the Basic's which, will challenge you to understand the forces that shape everyday life, cost of living, income, debt, and the systems most people never question. Together, these works form a single message: the future is built by the person who decides to take control.

One choice, one page, one brick at a time. You've reached the end of this book. But you're stepping into a wider path, one designed to help you own your life, strengthen your relationships, increase your freedom, and walk into every season of your story with clarity and confidence.

This is only the beginning.